Life's BIG Little Moments

MOTHERS & DAUGHTERS

Life's BIG Little Moments

MOTHERS & DAUGHTERS

SUSAN K. HOM

PHOTOGRAPHY BY MICHELLE ABELOFF

STERLING

New York / London
www.sterlingpublishing.com

For my mother, Noel, with love,
and special hugs to Heather and her daughter Alice

STERLING and the distinctive Sterling logo are registered trademarks of
Sterling Publishing Co., Inc.

Library of Congress Cataloging-in-Publication Data

Hom, Susan K.
  Life's big little moments : mothers & daughters / Susan K. Hom ; photography by John Rios.
    p. cm.
  ISBN-13: 978-1-4027-4319-1
  ISBN-10: 1-4027-4319-X
 1. Mothers and daughters--Miscellanea.   I.
Title.
  HQ755.85.H6343 2007
  306.874'3--dc22

                                                            2006102597

10 9 8 7 6 5 4 3 2

Published by Sterling Publishing Co., Inc.
387 Park Avenue South, New York, NY 10016
Distributed in Canada by Sterling Publishing
c/o Canadian Manda Group, 165 Dufferin Street
Toronto, Ontario, Canada M6K 3H6
Distributed in the United Kingdom by GMC Distribution Services
Castle Place, 166 High Street, Lewes, East Sussex, England BN7 1XU
Distributed in Australia by Capricorn Link (Australia) Pty. Ltd.
P.O. Box 704, Windsor, NSW 2756, Australia

Printed in China
All rights reserved

Sterling ISBN-13: 978-1-4027-4319-1
        ISBN-10: 1-4027-4319-X

For information about custom editions, special sales, premium and
corporate purchases, please contact Sterling Special Sales Department
at 800-805-5489 or specialsales@sterlingpublishing.com.

Cover and interior design by 3+Co. (www.threeandco.com)

All photos by Michelle Abeloff except:
    pages 2 ,6, 9, 24, 36, 91: John Rios
    page 11: © Maxim Tupikov / shutterstock.com
    page 21: © Trout55 / shutterstock.com
    page 35 photo: © LWA-Dan Tardiff / CORBIS
    pages 46–47 photo: Elizabeth Daniel / Elizabeth Daniel Photography
    page 73 photo: Laura Henehan
    page 94 photo: Kevin Law

Introduction

Mothers and daughters are partners on life's winding journey.
During joyful or trying times, it is their strong, resilient love that
grounds them. They teach each other what it means to love
generously and to live patiently. It would be tempting to say that
daughters learn more from mothers, because mothers are older
and wiser, but in every moment, daughters and mothers are
learning important life lessons from each other.

Each day is a new adventure. Mothers learn to appreciate simple
joys like spontaneous kisses and nightly storytime. Daughters
learn to boldly try new things and learn from their mistakes.
They learn how to encourage, forgive, and comfort each other.
They learn to appreciate each other's unique qualities.
In all of life's BIG little moments, mothers and daughters
remind each other that they are beautiful and deeply loved.

Mothers teach daughters

that hugs are precious.

Daughters inspire mothers

to delight in everyday moments.

Daughters show mothers

the importance of
slowing down sometimes.

Mothers encourage daughters

to embrace their talents.

Daughters remind mothers

that a smile can brighten any day.

Mothers make daughters giggle

with lots of funny faces.

Mothers heal daughters' boo-boos

with their special kisses.

Daughters teach mothers

to go with the flow.

Mothers teach daughters

how to be cautious while taking chances.

Daughters teach mothers

to be spontaneous.

Mothers help daughters

discover the power of their imagination.

Daughters teach mothers

that storytime is magical.

Mothers reassure daughters

that they are special.

Daughters teach mothers

the healing power of comforting words.

Mothers tell daughters

that they can accomplish anything.

Daughters inspire mothers

to relish the simple things in life.

Daughters remind mothers

that stuffed animals are
more than toys—they're buddies.

Mothers show daughters

that quiet time is important.

Mothers teach daughters

about true beauty.

Daughters show mothers

how to find joy in big *and* little moments.

Daughters teach mothers

how to heal a disappointed heart.

Mothers show daughters

that they are deeply loved.

Mothers show daughters

that they are safe with many tight hugs.

Daughters teach mothers

to enjoy the softness of a baby's cheek.

Mothers pass along to daughters

a love for the beauty around them.

Daughters teach mothers

to take time for personal reflection.

Mothers teach daughters

that the horizon stretches far and wide.

Daughters help mothers

treasure breathtaking moments.

Mothers encourage daughters

to be confident women.

Daughters teach mothers

that each day has many blessings.

Mothers show daughters

how to be a good friend.

Daughters teach mothers

to cherish intimate conversations.

Mothers help daughters

as they climb to new heights.

Daughters teach mothers

that life is an exciting adventure.

Mothers encourage daughters

to take life in small steps.

Daughters teach mothers

to rejoice in each milestone.

Daughters teach mothers

to not take things too seriously.

Mothers guide daughters

through life's ups and downs.

Mothers reassure daughters

that they will always be there for them.

Daughters comfort mothers

with affectionate hugs.

Mothers teach daughters

that they are works of art.

Daughters teach mothers

that one kiss isn't enough.

Mothers show daughters

how to forgive and move on.

Daughters teach mothers

that they both possess extraordinary love.

Mothers encourage daughters

to look for the best in people.

Daughters give mothers

many spontaneous kisses.

Daughters remind mothers

that laughter cures all.

Mothers encourage daughters

to look at things from different perspectives.

Mothers encourage daughters

to share their feelings.

Daughters teach mothers

to be good listeners.

Mothers encourage daughters

to be curious about everything.

Daughters teach mothers

that hearing "I love you"

is music to their ears.

Mothers inspire daughters

to unleash their creativity.

Daughters inspire mothers

to try new ways of doing things.

Mothers teach daughters

that tiaras go with everything.

Daughters show mothers

how to be young at heart.

Mothers teach daughters

to never lose their sense of wonder.

Daughters inspire mothers

to pursue their dreams.

Mothers introduce daughters

to the heavenly scent of flowers.

Daughters remind mothers

that miracles happen every day.

Mothers encourage daughters

to be independent.

Daughters teach mothers

that it's OK to let go.

Daughters teach mothers

the art of having fun.

Mothers catch daughters

when they fall.

Mothers teach daughters

that they belong.

Daughters remind mothers

that naps are wonderful.

Mothers teach daughters

that they are not alone.

Daughters teach mothers

how to have a gentle heart.

Mothers inspire daughters

to shine brightly.

Daughters remind mothers

to not be afraid of making mistakes.

Mothers show daughters

how to handle life's ebbs and flows.

Daughters remind mothers

how to savor the sand between their toes.

Mothers teach daughters

to be proud of being a woman.

Daughters inspire mothers

to live each day with courage and love.

Daughters teach mothers

to enjoy girl time, especially hair braiding.

Mothers teach daughters

that they are beautiful—just the way they are.

Mothers teach daughters

that they are treasures.

Daughters inspire mothers

to giggle often.

Mothers help daughters

persevere during tough times.

Daughters remind mothers

how to be content in all situations.

Mothers teach daughters

that they are full of great potential.

Daughters teach mothers

to celebrate each other's

similarities and differences.

Mothers reassure daughters

that they don't need to be perfect.

Daughters encourage mothers

to be silly.

Mothers teach daughters

how to love their new family.

Daughters teach mothers

to live with hope in a bright future.

Mothers teach daughters that

goofiness and bubbles go hand in hand.

Daughters remind mothers

to act like kids every now and then.

Mothers teach daughters how

to be the belle of the ball.

Daughters remind mothers that

the icing is the best part.